CW00864696

Gratitude
Journal
For Girls

Start Your Day With Gratitude

This Book
Belogs To

by Greer Dawson

SUN MON TUE WED THU FRI SAT

DATE
____/____/____

Today I am Thankful For:

_____

_____

_____

_____

Someone Who I Thanked Today:

_____

_____

Happiness
Scale

Write or draw about something
that made you laugh today

SUN MON TUE WED THU FRI SAT

DATE
____/____/____

Today I am Grateful for:

_____
_____
_____
_____
_____

Something Awesome That Happened Today:

_____
_____
_____

Happiness
Scale

Draw or write about your today's
act of gratitude

SUN MON TUE WED THU FRI SAT ____/____/____

Something great that happened today:

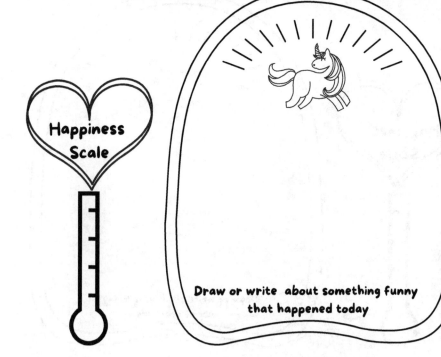

Happiness Scale

Draw or write about something funny
that happened today

SUN MON TUE WED THU FRI SAT ____/____/____

Positive thoughts of the day:

_____

_____

_____

_____

Write the names of the people you are grateful for:

_____

_____

_____

Happiness Scale

Write or draw about a moment
you really enjoyed today

Kindness Begins With Me

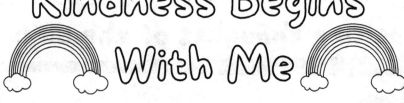

Pick up litter

Give a compliment

Leave someone a kind note

Write a positive note to a classmate

Hold the door open for someone

Donate old books or toys

Forgive someone's mistake

Do a chore for your sibling or Mom

Volunteer

Carry out a act of kindness, with no expectation of reward. Color them as you do them

SUN MON TUE WED THU FRI SAT

DATE

____/____/____

Today I am Thankful For:

_____

_____

_____

_____

Someone Who I Thanked Today:

_____

_____

Happiness
Scale

Write or draw about something
that made you laugh today

SUN MON TUE WED THU FRI SAT

DATE
____/____/____

Today I am Grateful for:

_____
_____
_____
_____
_____

Something Awesome That Happened Today:

_____
_____
_____

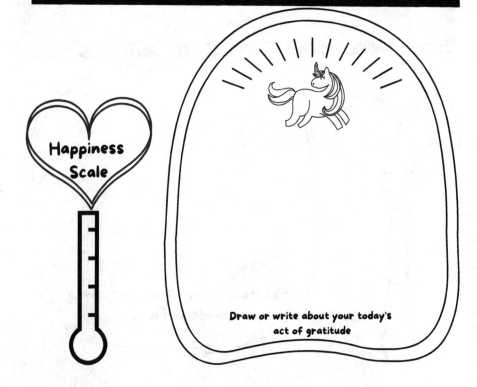

Happiness
Scale

Draw or write about your today's
act of gratitude

SUN MON TUE WED THU FRI SAT ____/____/____

Something great that happened today:

Happiness Scale

Draw or write about something funny
that happened today

SUN MON TUE WED THU FRI SAT ____/____/____

Positive thoughts of the day:

_____

_____

_____

_____

Write the names of the people you are grateful for:

_____

_____

_____

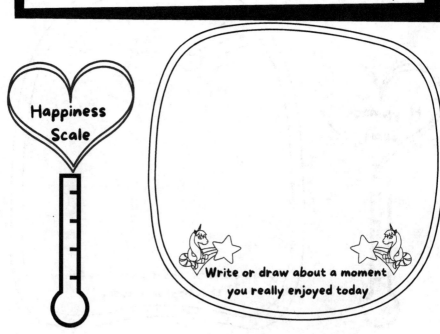

Happiness
Scale

Write or draw about a moment
you really enjoyed today

Kindness Begins With Me

Pick up litter

Give a compliment

Leave someone a kind note

Write a positive note to a classmate

Hold the door open for someone

Donate old books or toys

Forgive someone's mistake

Do a chore for your sibling or Mom

Volunteer

Carry out a act of kindness, with no expectation of reward. Color them as you do them

SUN MON TUE WED THU FRI SAT

Today I am Thankful For:

_____

_____

_____

_____

Someone Who I Thanked Today:

_____

_____

Happiness
Scale

Write or draw about something
that made you laugh today

SUN MON TUE WED THU FRI SAT

DATE
____/____/____

Today I am Grateful for:

_____
_____
_____
_____
_____

Something Awesome That Happened Today:

_____
_____
_____

Happiness Scale

Draw or write about your today's
act of gratitude

SUN MON TUE WED THU FRI SAT   ____/____/____

Something great that happened today:

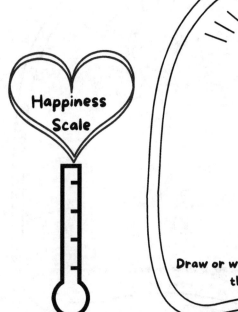

Happiness
Scale

Draw or write about something funny
that happened today

SUN MON TUE WED THU FRI SAT   ____/____/____

Positive thoughts of the day:

_____

_____

_____

_____

Write the names of the people you are grateful for:

_____

_____

_____

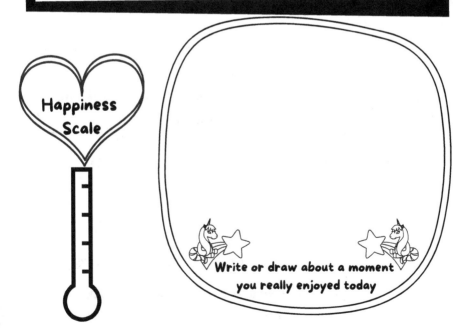

Happiness
Scale

Write or draw about a moment
you really enjoyed today

Kindness Begins With Me

Pick up litter

Give a compliment

Leave someone a kind note

Write a positive note to a classmate

Hold the door open for someone

Donate old books or toys

Forgive someone's mistake

Do a chore for your sibling or Mom

Volunteer

Carry out a act of kindness,
with no expectation of reward.
Color them as you do them

SUN MON TUE WED THU FRI SAT

DATE
____/____/____

Today I am Thankful For:

_____

_____

_____

_____

Someone Who I Thanked Today:

_____

_____

Happiness Scale

Write or draw about something
that made you laugh today

SUN MON TUE WED THU FRI SAT

Today I am Grateful for:

_____
_____
_____
_____
_____

Something Awesome That Happened Today:

_____
_____
_____

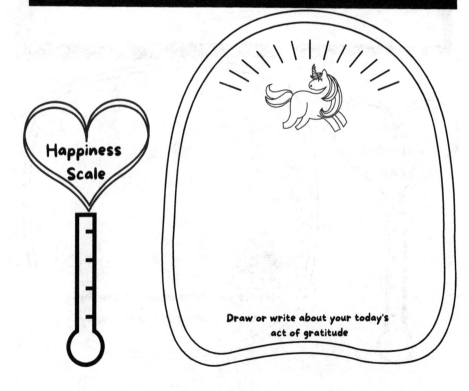

Happiness Scale

Draw or write about your today's act of gratitude

SUN MON TUE WED THU FRI SAT ____/____/____

Something great that happened today:

Happiness Scale

Draw or write about something funny
that happened today

SUN MON TUE WED THU FRI SAT ____/____/____

Positive thoughts of the day:

_____

_____

_____

_____

Write the names of the people you are grateful for:

_____

_____

_____

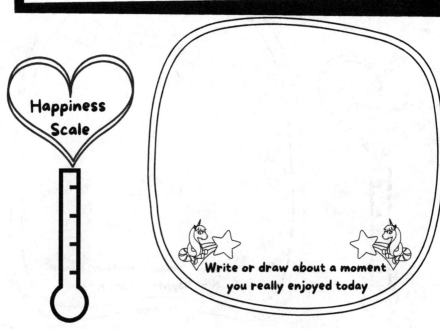

Happiness Scale

Write or draw about a moment
you really enjoyed today

Kindness Begins With Me

Pick up litter

Give a compliment

Leave someone a kind note

Write a positive note to a classmate

Hold the door open for someone

Donate old books or toys

Forgive someone's mistake

Do a chore for your sibling or Mom

Volunteer

Carry out a act of kindness, with no expectation of reward. Color them as you do them

SUN MON TUE WED THU FRI SAT

DATE
____/____/____

Today I am Thankful For:

_____

_____

_____

_____

Someone Who I Thanked Today:

_____

_____

Happiness
Scale

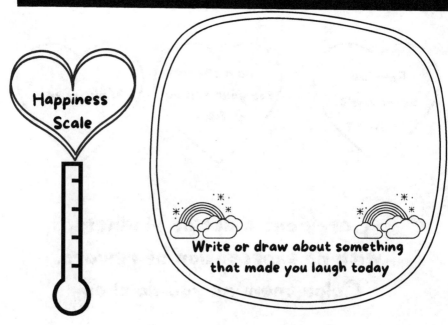

Write or draw about something
that made you laugh today

SUN MON TUE WED THU FRI SAT

DATE
____/____/____

Today I am Grateful for:

_____
_____
_____
_____
_____

Something Awesome That Happened Today:

_____
_____
_____

Happiness
Scale

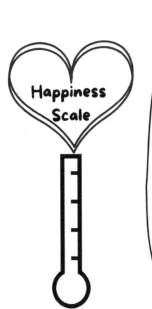

Draw or write about your today's
act of gratitude

SUN MON TUE WED THU FRI SAT ____/____/____

Something great that happened today:

Happiness
Scale

Draw or write about something funny
that happened today

SUN MON TUE WED THU FRI SAT ____/____/____

Positive thoughts of the day:

_____

_____

_____

_____

Write the names of the people you are grateful for:

_____

_____

_____

Happiness Scale

Write or draw about a moment
you really enjoyed today

Kindness Begins With Me

Pick up litter

Give a compliment

Leave someone a kind note

Write a positive note to a classmate

Hold the door open for someone

Donate old books or toys

Forgive someone's mistake

Do a chore for your sibling or Mom

Volunteer

Carry out a act of kindness,
with no expectation of reward.
Color them as you do them

SUN MON TUE WED THU FRI SAT

Today I am Thankful For:

_____

_____

_____

_____

Someone Who I Thanked Today:

_____

_____

Happiness Scale

Write or draw about something
that made you laugh today

SUN MON TUE WED THU FRI SAT

DATE
____/____/____

Today I am Grateful for:

_____
_____
_____
_____
_____

Something Awesome That Happened Today:

_____
_____
_____

Happiness
Scale

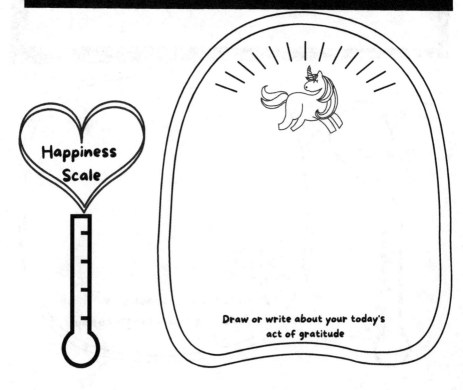

Draw or write about your today's
act of gratitude

SUN MON TUE WED THU FRI SAT ____/____/____

Something great that happened today:

Happiness Scale

Draw or write about something funny
that happened today

SUN MON TUE WED THU FRI SAT   ____/____/____

Positive thoughts of the day:

_____

_____

_____

_____

Write the names of the people you are grateful for:

_____

_____

_____

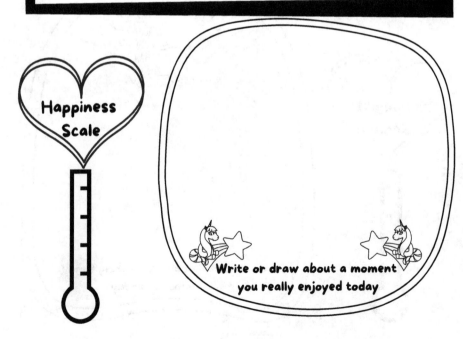

Happiness
Scale

Write or draw about a moment
you really enjoyed today

Kindness Begins With Me

Pick up litter

Give a compliment

Leave someone a kind note

Write a positive note to a classmate

Hold the door open for someone

Donate old books or toys

Forgive someone's mistake

Do a chore for your sibling or Mom

Volunteer

Carry out a act of kindness, with no expectation of reward. Color them as you do them

SUN MON TUE WED THU FRI SAT

Today I am Thankful For:

_____

_____

_____

_____

Someone Who I Thanked Today:

_____

_____

Happiness Scale

Write or draw about something
that made you laugh today

SUN MON TUE WED THU FRI SAT

Today I am Grateful for:

_____
_____
_____
_____
_____

Something Awesome That Happened Today:

_____
_____
_____

Happiness Scale

Draw or write about your today's act of gratitude

SUN MON TUE WED THU FRI SAT   ____/____/____

Something great that happened today:

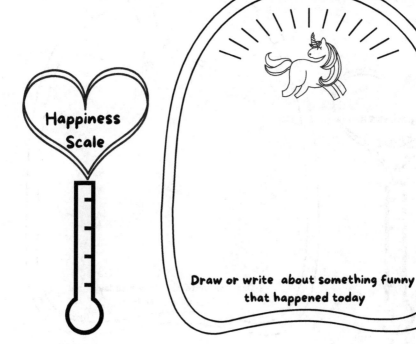

Happiness
Scale

Draw or write about something funny
that happened today

SUN MON TUE WED THU FRI SAT   ____/____/____

Positive thoughts of the day:

_____

_____

_____

_____

Write the names of the people you are grateful for:

_____

_____

_____

Happiness
Scale

Write or draw about a moment
you really enjoyed today

Kindness Begins With Me

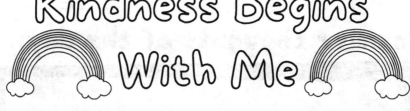

Pick up litter

Give a compliment

Leave someone a kind note

Write a positive note to a classmate

Hold the door open for someone

Donate old books or toys

Forgive someone's mistake

Do a chore for your sibling or Mom

Volunteer

Carry out a act of kindness, with no expectation of reward. Color them as you do them

SUN MON TUE WED THU FRI SAT

DATE
____/____/____

Today I am Thankful For:

_____

_____

_____

_____

Someone Who I Thanked Today:

_____

_____

Happiness
Scale

Write or draw about something
that made you laugh today

SUN MON TUE WED THU FRI SAT ____/____/____

Something great that happened today:

_____
_____
_____
_____
_____
_____
_____
_____

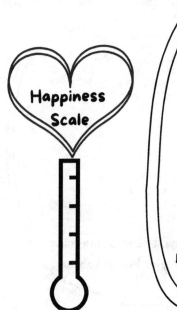

Happiness Scale

Draw or write about something funny
that happened today

SUN MON TUE WED THU FRI SAT ____/____/____

Positive thoughts of the day:

_____

_____

_____

_____

Write the names of the people you are grateful for:

_____

_____

_____

Happiness
Scale

Write or draw about a moment
you really enjoyed today

Kindness Begins With Me

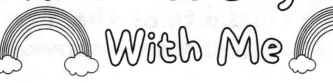

Pick up litter

Give a compliment

Leave someone a kind note

Write a positive note to a classmate

Hold the door open for someone

Donate old books or toys

Forgive someone's mistake

Do a chore for your sibling or Mom

Volunteer

Carry out a act of kindness, with no expectation of reward. Color them as you do them

Today I am Thankful For:

_____

_____

_____

_____

Someone Who I Thanked Today:

_____

_____

Happiness
Scale

Write or draw about something
that made you laugh today

Today I am Grateful for:

_____
_____
_____
_____
_____

Something Awesome That Happened Today:

_____
_____
_____

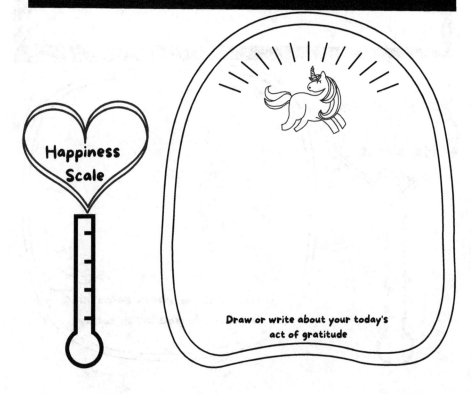

Happiness
Scale

Draw or write about your today's
act of gratitude

SUN MON TUE WED THU FRI SAT ____/____/____

Something great that happened today:

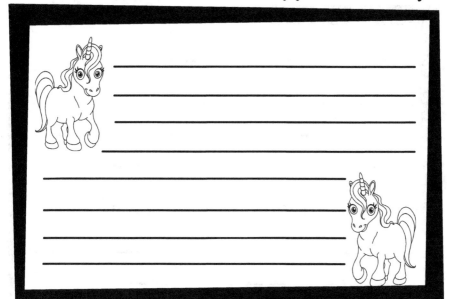

Happiness Scale

Draw or write about something funny that happened today

SUN MON TUE WED THU FRI SAT   ____/____/____

Positive thoughts of the day:

_____

_____

_____

_____

Write the names of the people you are grateful for:

_____

_____

_____

Happiness
Scale

Write or draw about a moment
you really enjoyed today

Kindness Begins With Me

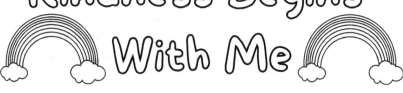

Pick up litter

Give a compliment

Leave someone a kind note

Write a positive note to a classmate

Hold the door open for someone

Donate old books or toys

Forgive someone's mistake

Do a chore for your sibling or Mom

Volunteer

Carry out a act of kindness,
with no expectation of reward.
Color them as you do them

SUN MON TUE WED THU FRI SAT

DATE

____/____/____

Today I am Thankful For:

_____

_____

_____

_____

Someone Who I Thanked Today:

_____

_____

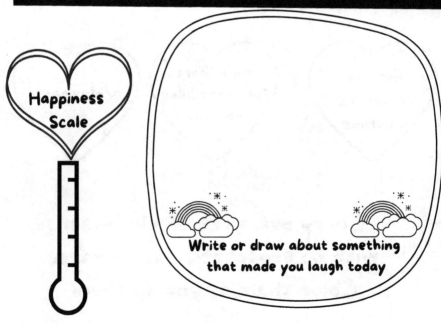

Happiness Scale

Write or draw about something that made you laugh today

SUN MON TUE WED THU FRI SAT

Today I am Grateful for:

_____
_____
_____
_____
_____

Something Awesome That Happened Today:

_____
_____
_____

Happiness Scale

Draw or write about your today's
act of gratitude

SUN MON TUE WED THU FRI SAT ____/____/____

Something great that happened today:

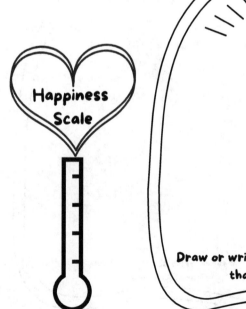

Happiness Scale

Draw or write about something funny that happened today

SUN MON TUE WED THU FRI SAT   ____/____/____

Positive thoughts of the day:

_____

_____

_____

_____

Write the names of the people you are grateful for:

_____

_____

_____

Happiness
Scale

Write or draw about a moment
you really enjoyed today

Kindness Begins With Me

Pick up litter

Give a compliment

Leave someone a kind note

Write a positive note to a classmate

Hold the door open for someone

Donate old books or toys

Forgive someone's mistake

Do a chore for your sibling or Mom

Volunteer

Carry out a act of kindness, with no expectation of reward. Color them as you do them

SUN MON TUE WED THU FRI SAT

DATE
____/____/____

Today I am Thankful For:

_____

_____

_____

_____

Someone Who I Thanked Today:

_____

_____

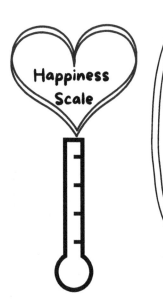

Happiness
Scale

Write or draw about something
that made you laugh today

SUN MON TUE WED THU FRI SAT

DATE
____/____/____

Today I am Grateful for:

_____

_____

_____

_____

_____

Something Awesome That Happened Today:

_____

_____

_____

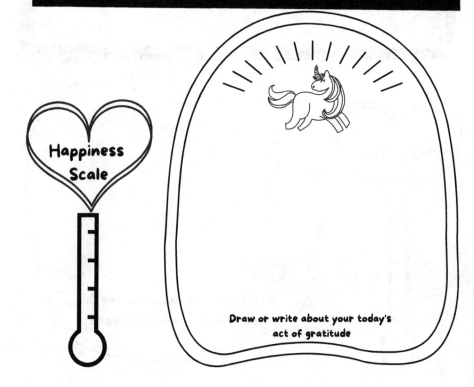

Happiness Scale

Draw or write about your today's act of gratitude

SUN MON TUE WED THU FRI SAT ____/____/____

Something great that happened today:

Happiness Scale

Draw or write about something funny
that happened today

SUN   MON   TUE   WED   THU   FRI   SAT   ____/____/____

Positive thoughts of the day:

_____

_____

_____

_____

Write the names of the people you are grateful for:

_____

_____

_____

Happiness Scale

Write or draw about a moment
you really enjoyed today

Kindness Begins With Me

Pick up litter

Give a compliment

Leave someone a kind note

Write a positive note to a classmate

Hold the door open for someone

Donate old books or toys

Forgive someone's mistake

Do a chore for your sibling or Mom

Volunteer

Carry out a act of kindness, with no expectation of reward. Color them as you do them

SUN MON TUE WED THU FRI SAT

DATE

____/____/____

Today I am Thankful For:

_____

_____

_____

_____

Someone Who I Thanked Today:

_____

_____

Happiness
Scale

Write or draw about something
that made you laugh today

SUN MON TUE WED THU FRI SAT

DATE

____/____/____

Today I am Grateful for:

_____

_____

_____

_____

_____

Something Awesome That Happened Today:

_____

_____

_____

Happiness
Scale

Draw or write about your today's
act of gratitude

SUN   MON   TUE   WED   THU   FRI   SAT   ____/____/____

Something great that happened today:

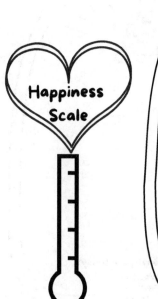

Happiness
Scale

Draw or write about something funny
that happened today

SUN MON TUE WED THU FRI SAT ____/____/____

Positive thoughts of the day:

_____

_____

_____

_____

Write the names of the people you are grateful for:

_____

_____

_____

Happiness Scale

Write or draw about a moment
you really enjoyed today

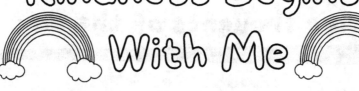

Kindness Begins With Me

Pick up litter

Give a compliment

Leave someone a kind note

Write a positive note to a classmate

Hold the door open for someone

Donate old books or toys

Forgive someone's mistake

Do a chore for your sibling or Mom

Volunteer

Carry out a act of kindness, with no expectation of reward. Color them as you do them

SUN MON TUE WED THU FRI SAT

DATE
____/____/____

Today I am Thankful For:

_____

_____

_____

_____

Someone Who I Thanked Today:

_____

_____

Happiness
Scale

Write or draw about something
that made you laugh today

SUN MON TUE WED THU FRI SAT

DATE
____/____/____

Today I am Grateful for:

_____
_____
_____

_____
_____

Something Awesome That Happened Today:

_____
_____
_____

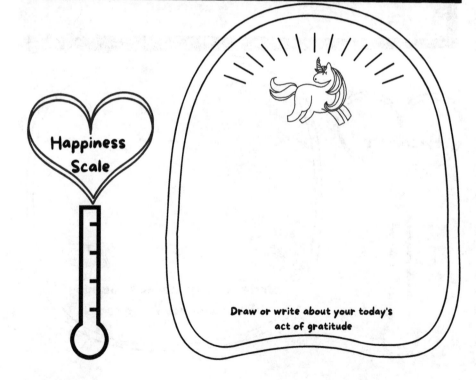

Happiness
Scale

Draw or write about your today's
act of gratitude

SUN MON TUE WED THU FRI SAT ____/____/____

Something great that happened today:

Happiness
Scale

Draw or write about something funny
that happened today

SUN MON TUE WED THU FRI SAT

____/____/____

Positive thoughts of the day:

_____

_____

_____

_____

Write the names of the people you are grateful for:

_____

_____

_____

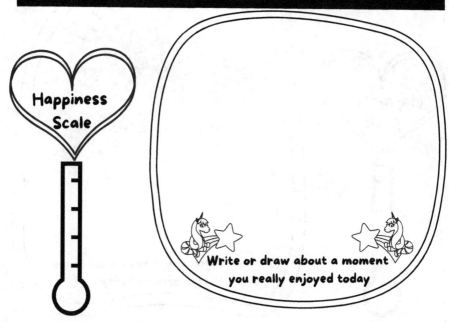

Happiness Scale

Write or draw about a moment
you really enjoyed today

Kindness Begins With Me

Pick up litter

Give a compliment

Leave someone a kind note

Write a positive note to a classmate

Hold the door open for someone

Donate old books or toys

Forgive someone's mistake

Do a chore for your sibling or Mom

Volunteer

Carry out a act of kindness, with no expectation of reward. Color them as you do them

SUN MON TUE WED THU FRI SAT

DATE
____/____/____

Today I am Thankful For:

_____

_____

_____

Someone Who I Thanked Today:

_____

_____

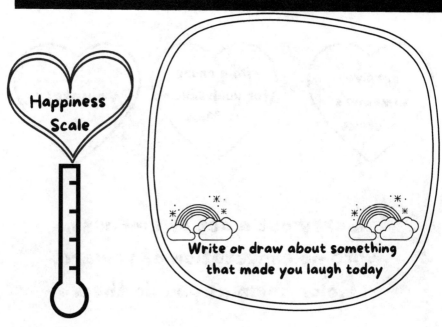

Happiness
Scale

Write or draw about something
that made you laugh today

SUN MON TUE WED THU FRI SAT

DATE

____/____/____

Today I am Grateful for:

_____
_____
_____
_____
_____

Something Awesome That Happened Today:

_____
_____
_____

Happiness Scale

Draw or write about your today's
act of gratitude

SUN MON TUE WED THU FRI SAT   ____/____/____

Something great that happened today:

Happiness
Scale

Draw or write about something funny
that happened today

SUN MON TUE WED THU FRI SAT   ____/____/____

Positive thoughts of the day:

_____

_____

_____

_____

Write the names of the people you are grateful for:

_____

_____

_____

Happiness
Scale

Write or draw about a moment
you really enjoyed today

Kindness Begins With Me

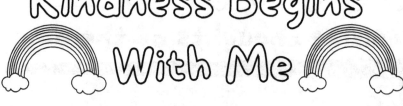

Pick up litter

Give a compliment

Leave someone a kind note

Write a positive note to a classmate

Hold the door open for someone

Donate old books or toys

Forgive someone's mistake

Do a chore for your sibling or Mom

Volunteer

Carry out a act of kindness,
with no expectation of reward.
Color them as you do them

SUN MON TUE WED THU FRI SAT

DATE
____/____/____

Today I am Thankful For:

_____

_____

_____

_____

Someone Who I Thanked Today:

_____

_____

Happiness
Scale

Write or draw about something
that made you laugh today

SUN MON TUE WED THU FRI SAT

DATE
____/____/____

Today I am Grateful for:

_____
_____
_____
_____
_____

Something Awesome That Happened Today:

_____
_____
_____

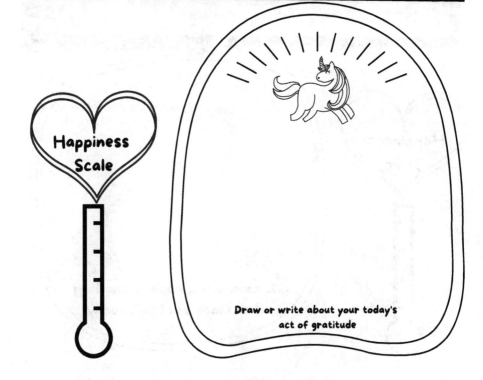

Happiness Scale

Draw or write about your today's
act of gratitude

SUN MON TUE WED THU FRI SAT   ____/____/____

Something great that happened today:

Happiness Scale

Draw or write about something funny
that happened today

SUN MON TUE WED THU FRI SAT   ____/____/____

Positive thoughts of the day:

_____

_____

_____

_____

Write the names of the people you are grateful for:

_____

_____

_____

Happiness
Scale

Write or draw about a moment
you really enjoyed today

Kindness Begins With Me

Pick up litter

Give a compliment

Leave someone a kind note

Write a positive note to a classmate

Hold the door open for someone

Donate old books or toys

Forgive someone's mistake

Do a chore for your sibling or Mom

Volunteer

Carry out a act of kindness, with no expectation of reward. Color them as you do them

SUN MON TUE WED THU FRI SAT

DATE

____/____/____

Today I am Thankful For:

_____

_____

_____

_____

Someone Who I Thanked Today:

_____

_____

Happiness Scale

Write or draw about something that made you laugh today

SUN MON TUE WED THU FRI SAT

DATE
____/____/____

Today I am Grateful for:

_____
_____
_____
_____
_____

Something Awesome That Happened Today:

_____
_____
_____

Happiness
Scale

Draw or write about your today's
act of gratitude

SUN   MON   TUE   WED   THU   FRI   SAT   ____/____/____

Something great that happened today:

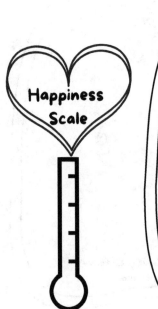

Happiness
Scale

Draw or write about something funny
that happened today

SUN MON TUE WED THU FRI SAT   ____/____/____

Positive thoughts of the day:

_____

_____

_____

_____

Write the names of the people you are grateful for:

_____

_____

_____

Happiness
Scale

Write or draw about a moment
you really enjoyed today

Kindness Begins With Me

Pick up litter

Give a compliment

Leave someone a kind note

Write a positive note to a classmate

Hold the door open for someone

Donate old books or toys

Forgive someone's mistake

Do a chore for your sibling or Mom

Volunteer

Carry out a act of kindness, with no expectation of reward. Color them as you do them

SUN MON TUE WED THU FRI SAT

Today I am Thankful For:

_____

_____

_____

_____

Someone Who I Thanked Today:

_____

_____

Happiness
Scale

Write or draw about something
that made you laugh today

SUN MON TUE WED THU FRI SAT

DATE

____/____/____

Today I am Grateful for:

_____
_____
_____

_____

_____

Something Awesome That Happened Today:

_____

_____

_____

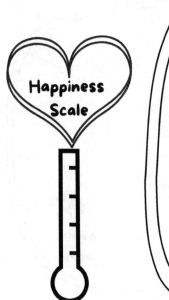

Happiness Scale

Draw or write about your today's act of gratitude

SUN MON TUE WED THU FRI SAT ____/____/____

Something great that happened today:

Happiness Scale

Draw or write about something funny
that happened today

SUN MON TUE WED THU FRI SAT

____/____/____

Positive thoughts of the day:

_____

_____

_____

_____

Write the names of the people you are grateful for:

_____

_____

_____

Happiness Scale

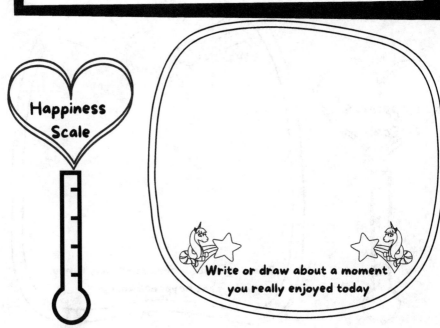

Write or draw about a moment
you really enjoyed today

Kindness Begins With Me

Pick up litter

Give a compliment

Leave someone a kind note

Write a positive note to a classmate

Hold the door open for someone

Donate old books or toys

Forgive someone's mistake

Do a chore for your sibling or Mom

Volunteer

Carry out a act of kindness, with no expectation of reward.
Color them as you do them

SUN MON TUE WED THU FRI SAT

DATE
____/____/____

Today I am Thankful For:

_____

_____

_____

_____

Someone Who I Thanked Today:

_____

_____

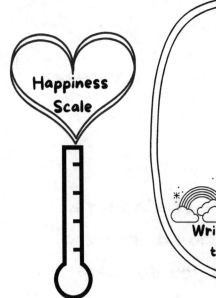

Happiness
Scale

Write or draw about something
that made you laugh today

SUN MON TUE WED THU FRI SAT

DATE

____/____/____

Today I am Grateful for:

_____

_____

_____

_____

_____

Something Awesome That Happened Today:

_____

_____

_____

Happiness
Scale

Draw or write about your today's
act of gratitude

SUN MON TUE WED THU FRI SAT ____/____/____

Something great that happened today:

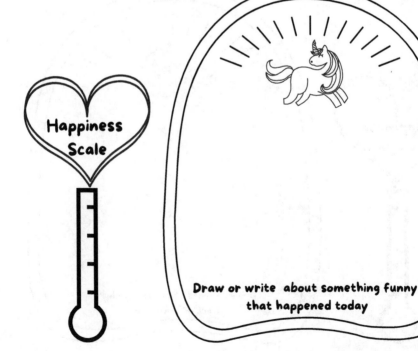

Happiness
Scale

Draw or write about something funny
that happened today

SUN MON TUE WED THU FRI SAT ____/____/____

Positive thoughts of the day:

_____

_____

_____

_____

Write the names of the people you are grateful for:

_____

_____

_____

Happiness Scale

Write or draw about a moment you really enjoyed today

Kindness Begins With Me

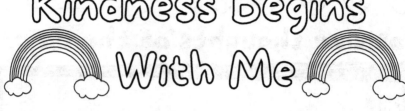

Pick up litter

Give a compliment

Leave someone a kind note

Write a positive note to a classmate

Hold the door open for someone

Donate old books or toys

Forgive someone's mistake

Do a chore for your sibling or Mom

Volunteer

Carry out a act of kindness, with no expectation of reward. Color them as you do them

SUN MON TUE WED THU FRI SAT

Today I am Thankful For:

_____

_____

_____

_____

Someone Who I Thanked Today:

_____

_____

Happiness Scale

Write or draw about something
that made you laugh today

SUN MON TUE WED THU FRI SAT

DATE

____/____/____

Today I am Grateful for:

_____
_____
_____
_____
_____

Something Awesome That Happened Today:

_____
_____
_____

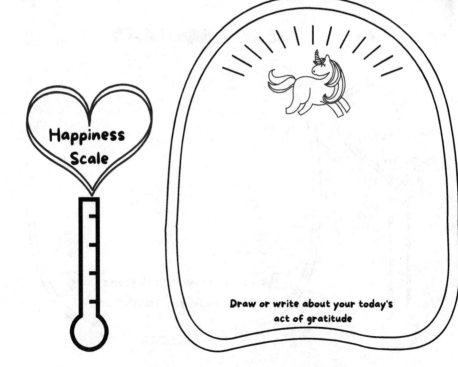

Happiness
Scale

**Draw or write about your today's
act of gratitude**

SUN MON TUE WED THU FRI SAT   ____/____/____

Something great that happened today:

Happiness Scale

Draw or write about something funny
that happened today

SUN MON TUE WED THU FRI SAT ____/____/____

Positive thoughts of the day:

_____

_____

_____

_____

Write the names of the people you are grateful for:

_____

_____

_____

Happiness
Scale

Write or draw about a moment
you really enjoyed today

Kindness Begins With Me

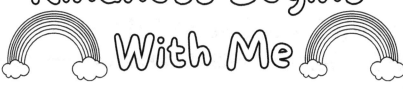

Pick up litter

Give a compliment

Leave someone a kind note

Write a positive note to a classmate

Hold the door open for someone

Donate old books or toys

Forgive someone's mistake

Do a chore for your sibling or Mom

Volunteer

Carry out a act of kindness, with no expectation of reward. Color them as you do them

SUN MON TUE WED THU FRI SAT

DATE
____/____/____

Today I am Thankful For:

_____

_____

_____

_____

Someone Who I Thanked Today:

_____

_____

Happiness
Scale

Write or draw about something
that made you laugh today

SUN MON TUE WED THU FRI SAT

DATE
____/____/____

Today I am Grateful for:

_____
_____
_____
_____
_____

Something Awesome That Happened Today:

_____
_____
_____

Happiness Scale

Draw or write about your today's act of gratitude

SUN MON TUE WED THU FRI SAT ____/____/____

Something great that happened today:

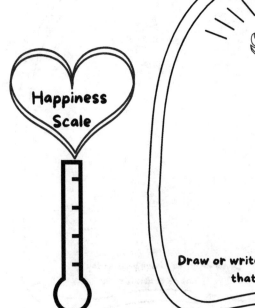

Happiness Scale

Draw or write about something funny
that happened today

SUN MON TUE WED THU FRI SAT ____/____/____

Positive thoughts of the day:

Write the names of the people you are grateful for:

Happiness
Scale

Write or draw about a moment
you really enjoyed today

Kindness Begins With Me

Pick up litter

Give a compliment

Leave someone a kind note

Write a positive note to a classmate

Hold the door open for someone

Donate old books or toys

Forgive someone's mistake

Do a chore for your sibling or Mom

Volunteer

Carry out a act of kindness, with no expectation of reward. Color them as you do them

SUN MON TUE WED THU FRI SAT

DATE
____/____/____

Today I am Thankful For:

_____

_____

_____

_____

Someone Who I Thanked Today:

_____

_____

Happiness
Scale

Write or draw about something
that made you laugh today

SUN MON TUE WED THU FRI SAT

DATE
____/____/____

Today I am Grateful for:

_____
_____
_____
_____
_____

Something Awesome That Happened Today:

_____
_____
_____

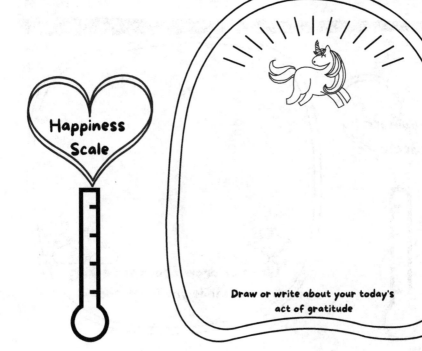

Happiness
Scale

Draw or write about your today's
act of gratitude

SUN MON TUE WED THU FRI SAT   ____/____/____

Something great that happened today:

_____

_____

_____

_____

_____

_____

_____

_____

Happiness
Scale

Draw or write about something funny
that happened today

SUN MON TUE WED THU FRI SAT _ _ _ _ / _ _ _ _ / _ _ _ _

Positive thoughts of the day:

_____

_____

_____

_____

Write the names of the people you are grateful for:

_____

_____

Happiness Scale

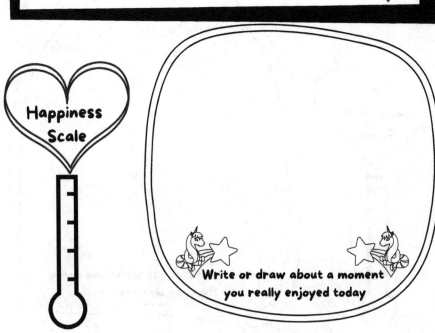

Write or draw about a moment you really enjoyed today

Kindness Begins With Me

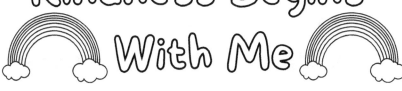

Pick up litter

Give a compliment

Leave someone a kind note

Write a positive note to a classmate

Hold the door open for someone

Donate old books or toys

Forgive someone's mistake

Do a chore for your sibling or Mom

Volunteer

Carry out a act of kindness, with no expectation of reward. Color them as you do them

SUN MON TUE WED THU FRI SAT

DATE
____/____/____

Today I am Thankful For:

_____

_____

_____

_____

Someone Who I Thanked Today:

_____

_____

Happiness Scale

Write or draw about something that made you laugh today

SUN MON TUE WED THU FRI SAT

DATE

____/____/____

Today I am Grateful for:

_____

_____

_____

_____

_____

Something Awesome That Happened Today:

_____

_____

_____

Happiness Scale

Draw or write about your today's
act of gratitude

SUN MON TUE WED THU FRI SAT ____/____/____

Something great that happened today:

Happiness Scale

Draw or write about something funny
that happened today

SUN MON TUE WED THU FRI SAT ____/____/____

Positive thoughts of the day:

_____

_____

_____

_____

Write the names of the people you are grateful for:

_____

_____

_____

Happiness
Scale

Write or draw about a moment
you really enjoyed today

Kindness Begins With Me

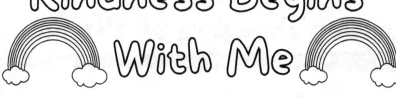

Pick up litter

Give a compliment

Leave someone a kind note

Write a positive note to a classmate

Hold the door open for someone

Donate old books or toys

Forgive someone's mistake

Do a chore for your sibling or Mom

Volunteer

Carry out a act of kindness, with no expectation of reward. Color them as you do them

SUN MON TUE WED THU FRI SAT

DATE
____/____/____

Today I am Thankful For:

_____

_____

_____

_____

Someone Who I Thanked Today:

_____

_____

Happiness
Scale

Write or draw about something
that made you laugh today

SUN MON TUE WED THU FRI SAT

DATE

____/____/____

Today I am Grateful for:

Something Awesome That Happened Today:

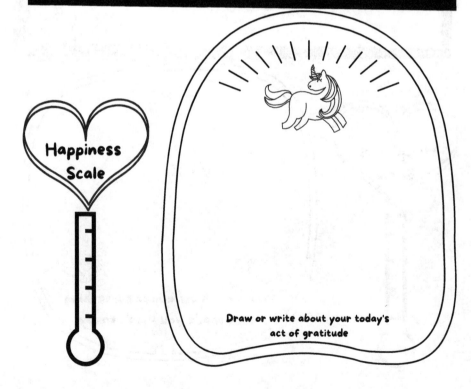

Happiness Scale

Draw or write about your today's
act of gratitude

SUN MON TUE WED THU FRI SAT   ____/____/____

Something great that happened today:

_____

_____

_____

_____

_____

_____

_____

Happiness Scale

Draw or write about something funny that happened today

SUN MON TUE WED THU FRI SAT ____/____/____

Positive thoughts of the day:

_____

_____

_____

_____

Write the names of the people you are grateful for:

_____

_____

_____

Happiness Scale

Write or draw about a moment you really enjoyed today

Kindness Begins With Me

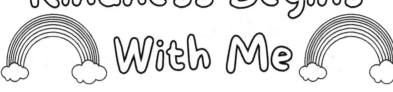

Pick up litter

Give a compliment

Leave someone a kind note

Write a positive note to a classmate

Hold the door open for someone

Donate old books or toys

Forgive someone's mistake

Do a chore for your sibling or Mom

Volunteer

Carry out a act of kindness, with no expectation of reward. Color them as you do them

SUN MON TUE WED THU FRI SAT

DATE

____/____/____

Today I am Thankful For:

_____

_____

_____

_____

Someone Who I Thanked Today:

_____

_____

Happiness
Scale

Write or draw about something
that made you laugh today

SUN **MON** **TUE** **WED** **THU** **FRI** **SAT**

DATE
____/____/____

Today I am Grateful for:

_____
_____
_____
_____
_____

Something Awesome That Happened Today:

_____
_____
_____

Happiness Scale

Draw or write about your today's
act of gratitude

SUN MON TUE WED THU FRI SAT ____/____/____

Something great that happened today:

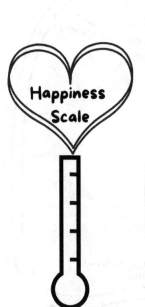

Happiness Scale

Draw or write about something funny
that happened today

SUN MON TUE WED THU FRI SAT ____/____/____

Positive thoughts of the day:

_____

_____

_____

_____

Write the names of the people you are grateful for:

_____

_____

_____

Happiness
Scale

Write or draw about a moment
you really enjoyed today

Kindness Begins With Me

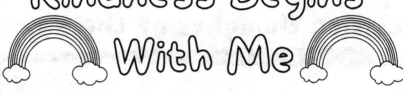

Pick up litter

Give a compliment

Leave someone a kind note

Write a positive note to a classmate

Hold the door open for someone

Donate old books or toys

Forgive someone's mistake

Do a chore for your sibling or Mom

Volunteer

Carry out a act of kindness, with no expectation of reward. Color them as you do them

We hope you enjoyed our book.

As a small family company, your feedback is very important to us.

Please let us know how you like our book at:

greer.dawson89@gmail.com

If you want to be up to date with the new books published, please let me know in a message and be one of the first people to have access to them.

CPSIA information can be obtained
at www.ICGtesting.com
Printed in the USA
LVHW081156170621
690182LV00018B/297

9 781446 157503